First Facts®

Spotlight on the Continents

SPOTLIGHT ON
ANTARCTICA

by A. R. Schaefer

CAPSTONE PRESS
a capstone imprint

First Facts is published by Capstone Press,
1710 Roe Crest Drive, North Mankato, Minnesota 56003.
www.capstonepub.com

 Books published by Capstone Press are manufactured with paper
containing at least 10 percent post-consumer waste.

Library of Congress Cataloging-in-Publication Data
Schaefer, A. R. (Adam Richard), 1976–
 Spotlight on Antarctica / by A. R. Schaefer.
    p. cm.—(First facts. Spotlight on the continents)
 Summary: "An introduction to Antarctica including climate, landforms, plants,
animals, and people"—Provided by publisher.
 Includes bibliographical references and index.
 ISBN 978-1-4296-6626-8 (library binding)
 1. Antarctica—Juvenile literature. I. Title.
 G863.S726 2011
 919.8'9—dc22
                                        2010037094

Editorial Credits
Lori Shores, editor; Gene Bentdahl, designer; Laura Manthe, production specialist

Photo Credits
Alamy/Lonely Planet Images/Grant Dixon, 13; Photoshot Holdings Ltd, 20
Creatas, 1
Dreamstime/Andrey Pavlov, 19; Darryn Schneider, 9
Getty Images Inc./National Geographic/Gordon Wiltsie, 7 (top)
Shutterstock/Armin Rose, 16; Gentoo Multimedia Ltd., 14; Map Resources, 7 (bottom);
    Nina B, cover; Volodymyr Goinyk, 18

Artistic Effects
Shutterstock/seed

Essential content terms are **bold** and are defined at the bottom of the page
where they first appear.

Printed in the United States of America in North Mankato, Minnesota.
062012   006797R

TABLE OF CONTENTS

Antarctica..5

Fast Facts about Antarctica 6

Climate 8

Landforms 11

Plants..12

Animals...15

People..17

Living in Antarctica......................................18

Antarctica and the World 21

Glossary..22

Read More 23

Internet Sites 23

Index 24

CONTINENTS OF THE WORLD

ARCTIC OCEAN

ASIA

NORTH AMERICA

EUROPE

ASIA

ATLANTIC OCEAN

AFRICA

PACIFIC OCEAN

EQUATOR

INDIAN OCEAN

SOUTH AMERICA

N W E S

AUSTRALIA

SOUTHERN OCEAN

ANTARCTICA

ANTARCTICA

Little land can be seen through the thick layer of ice that covers Antarctica. But this landmass is the world's fifth-largest **continent**. It covers about 5.4 million square miles (14 million square kilometers).

No one lives in Antarctica. But every year, thousands of people visit Antarctica to study this cold continent.

continent—one of Earth's seven large landmasses

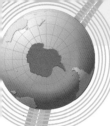

FAST FACTS ABOUT
ANTARCTICA

- **Population:** Between 1,000 and 4,500 people from many countries visit Antarctica each year.

- **Highest point:** Vinson Massif, 16,067 feet (4,897 meters) above sea level

- **Highest temperature ever recorded:** 59 degrees Fahrenheit (15 degrees Celsius)

- **Lowest temperature ever recorded:** minus 128.6 degrees Fahrenheit (minus 89.2 degrees Celsius)

VINSON MASSIF

VINSON MASSIF

CLIMATE

Antarctica has the coldest **climate** on Earth. During winter, temperatures drop to -94 °F (-70 °C). Even during summer, temperatures rarely rise above freezing.

Antarctica is also the world's driest place. Each year, only about 2 inches (5 centimeters) of snow falls. But snow has piled up in Antarctica for millions of years.

climate—the usual weather that occurs in a place

LANDFORMS OF ANTARTICA

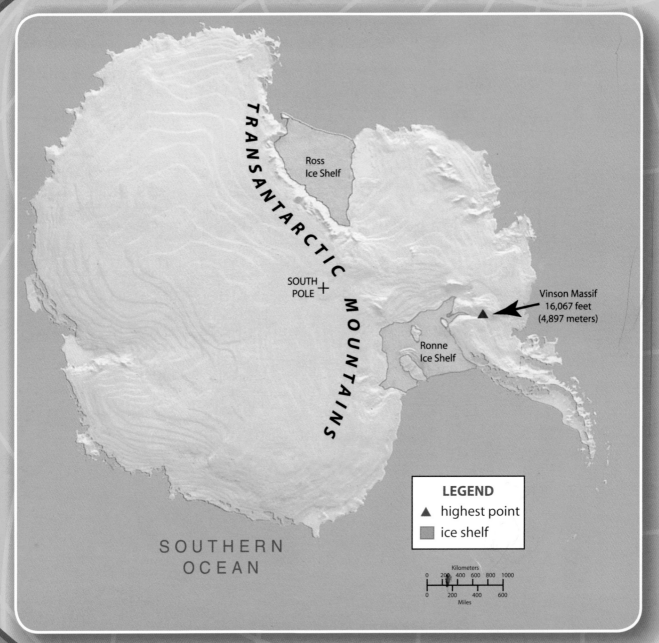

TRANSANTARCTIC MOUNTAINS

Ross Ice Shelf

SOUTH POLE +

Vinson Massif
16,067 feet
(4,897 meters)

Ronne Ice Shelf

SOUTHERN OCEAN

LEGEND
▲ highest point
■ ice shelf

Kilometers
0   200   400   600   800   1000
0   200   400   600
Miles

LANDFORMS

Ice isn't found only on Antarctica's land. Huge ice chunks float in the Southern Ocean around Antarctica. And large, flat **ice shelves** connect to Antarctica's coasts.

The Transantarctic Mountains divide Antarctica. The world's most southern point, the South Pole, is near these mountains.

ice shelf—a floating sheet of ice permanently attached to a landmass

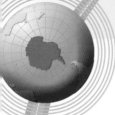

PLANTS

Few plants grow in Antarctica's cold climate. Most plants grow along Antarctica's snow-free coast. Antarctic hair grass and Antarctic pearlworts live on this warmer land. Green moss and orange **lichens** cover rocks. In summer, some snow melts, providing water to snow-covered **algae**.

lichen—a flat, mosslike plant that grows on trees and rocks

algae—small plants without roots or stems that grow in water or on damp surfaces

ANIMALS

Many ocean animals live in the water around Antarctica. Penguins and seals visit the icy land only to raise their young.

During summer, more than 40 types of birds nest on Antarctica. During the day, they fly over the Southern Ocean looking for fish to eat.

PEOPLE

Antarctica has no native people. But scientists from many countries do **research** in Antarctica. The scientists study Antarctica's plants, animals, and landforms.

About 4,500 researchers stay in Antarctica during the summer. During the cold winter, only about 1,000 people stay in Antarctica.

research—a study or investigation to learn new facts

LIVING IN ANTARCTICA

Life in Antarctica is harsh. Even in summer, the continent stays windy, dry, and cold. People need many layers of clothing to stay warm.

Scientists live at research stations in Antarctica. They grow vegetables inside **greenhouses**. But most food must be flown or shipped to this cold continent.

ANTARCTICA AND THE WORLD

People from all over the world are interested in Antarctica. The icy land holds clues about the world's history and future. Scientists test old ice sheets to learn about past climates. Ice sheets may also give scientists clues about the world's climate in the years ahead. Research in Antarctica may help solve future world problems.

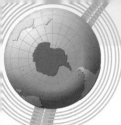

GLOSSARY

algae (AL-jee)—small plants without roots or stems that grow in water or on damp surfaces

climate (KLY-muht)—the usual weather that occurs in a place

continent (KAHN-tuh-nuhnt)—one of Earth's seven large land masses

greenhouse (GREEN-houss)—a warm building where plants can grow

ice shelf (EYESS SHELF)—a floating sheet of ice permanently attached to a landmass

lichen (LYE-ken)—a flat, mosslike plant that grows on trees and rocks

research (REE-surch)—a study or investigation to learn new facts

READ MORE

Friedman, Mel. *Antarctica.* A True Book. New York: Children's Press, 2009.

Meinking, Mary. *Who Counts the Penguins?: Working in Antarctica.* Wild Work. Chicago: Raintree, 2011.

INTERNET SITES

FactHound offers a safe, fun way to find Internet sites related to this book. All of the sites on FactHound have been researched by our staff.

Here's all you do:

Visit *www.facthound.com*

Type in this code: 9781429666268

Super-cool stuff! Check out projects, games and lots more at **www.capstonekids.com**

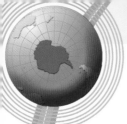

INDEX

animals, 15, 17

climate, 8, 12, 18, 21
clothing, 18

food, 19

highest point, 6

ice, 5, 11, 21
ice shelves, 11

landforms, 11, 17

people, 5, 17, 18, 21
plants, 12, 17
population, 6

research, 17, 21
researchers, 17
research stations, 19

scientists, 17, 19, 21
size, 5
snow, 8, 12
South Pole, 11

temperatures, 6, 8
Transantarctic
    Mountains, 11

Vinson Massif, 6